D0877771

LONG AFTER LAUDS

LONG AFTER LAUDS

Poems

Jeanine Hathaway

LONG AFTER LAUDS
Poems

Copyright © 2019 Jeanine Hathaway. All rights reserved. Except for brief quotations in critical publications or reviews, no part of this book may be reproduced in any manner without prior written permission from the publisher. Write: Permissions, Wipf and Stock Publishers, 199 W. 8th Ave., Suite 3, Eugene, OR 97401.

Poems from *The Ex-Nun Poems*. Copyright © 2011 by Jeanine Hathaway. Reprinted with the permission of The Permissions Company LLC on behalf of Finishing Line Press, www.finishinglinepress.com. All rights reserved.

Slant
An Imprint of Wipf and Stock Publishers
199 W. 8th Ave., Suite 3
Eugene, OR 97401

www.wipfandstock.com

HARDCOVER ISBN: 978-1-5326-8928-4
PAPERBACK ISBN: 978-1-5326-8929-1
EBOOK ISBN: 978-1-5326-8930-7

Cataloguing-in-Publication data:

Names: Hathaway, Jeanine.

Title: Long after lauds: poems. / Jeanine Hathaway.

Description: Eugene, OR: Slant, 2019.

Identifiers: ISBN 978-1-5326-8928-4 (hardcover) | ISBN 978-1-5326-8929-1 (paperback) | ISBN 978-1-5326-8930-7 (ebook)

Subjects: LCSH: Poetry. / American poetry—21st century.

Classification: PS3558.A746 L66 2019 (paperback) | PS3558.A746 (ebook)

Manufactured in the U.S.A.   06/12/19

For Charlotte, Beatrice, and Sadie

Contents

MAKING IT UP UNDER WATER

(*creation myth*)

This world's born from a trench, hot vent
in the depths. A bio-luminous bacterial

ballet, gravity free. Play begat jellyfish:
no bones, or brain, or blood. What in the

squid circulates is copper; a scrape seeps
not iron red but blue. Blood and tentacles,

the beginning of friction, sting, and ink.

DISAPPOINTMENTS

The gruff curator expects more of us, a tide
of schoolkids maybe after a long ride, bus rowdy,
to his makeshift sea lab, tanks cleaned. Terms
on the white-board wall color the language
of mollusk, cephalopod, sea star, anemone.

Only two of us show up, ambling along the beach,
our glasses smeared by sea spray and drizzle.
The man, heavy, bewhiskered Navy vet, bad back,
decides to withhold more than he'll teach. "Go on."
We're free, hands on, to poke inside the tubs.

Your fingertip sinks down a sea star's arm;
tube feet feel their wet way up to the foodless air.
My fingertip nettles an anemone, pink petaled
succulent, friction in the barbs. Stinging
nematocysts, they poison inedible me.

The curator from his stool across the lab grunts.
I head for the sink, touch nothing but soap and
scrub. All he'll hear from here on: a woman
his age washing, not clapping, not the brilliant
applause he'd spent the morning setting up for.

ICHTHYOLOGY

Hacked and sliced, a pile of salmon halves
rots in the parking lot at the river's mouth.
Orange and silver dinner for crows, part

installation, the Coho stare into tires, truck
bumpers. I stare into them: their bones
fallen combs, tails feathery, curling to

clumps. Flies swarm; the buzz is glued
to the asphalt. Not swimming, no flop or
fight—the meat's gone out of the argument.

I shovel them back into the river.
Let whitewater tear them apart. Make private
the shame of this flaying, pick them clean,

inarticulate. A spiny silence lies below a hook.
Let even their bones be as useful as prayer,
those fine lines that some would call the catch.

BEFORE ENTERING

"—5—6—7—8, and 1—" The dancers drum onstage
from the wings where they were before the downbeat,
that pre-historic moment, bandaged and flinching,
calloused, split, grinning—the tick-swish of soles
on bare wood; their presence shifts how light leaps
off the watch of the ex-nun's date. Such sound
bodies. Their backs, extraordinary overlaps
of muscle bound to bone. Contract/release,
land masses, ice floes break up, tectonics.
India ramming Asia there, under the scapula,
Himalayan scapula where legend says Doubting
Thomas spread the Gospel, a martyr in the shadow
of Everest or these wing-boned backs. It is
good news, the teaching: The dance does not begin
on the downbeat. You're already dancing
on the "—5—6—7—8, and—"

you enter with history. Getting comfortable,
the ex-nun tilts her chin, lowers her shoulders
barely covered by rose silk,
once covered by a white wool scapular, that
strip of habit worn between gown and cape.
Her hands flat under it, thumbs tucked
into her belt. Her body still, if nothing more,

her presentation inspired by—what?—a long
tradition of women, given. Diamonds now
at her ears and throat, hands, ungloved yet
folded. She understands medieval Eckhart's prayer
that God should rid him of God, as she could not at 25,
longing never to lose the idolatry, feeling it go:
the cloak; the headgear of wimple and guimpe;
veil, cape, tunic; sensible grandmother shoes.

She wonders: How could she or anyone dance and not
enter with history? How does gravity, the law of the present,
perfect the dancer? The stretch at the barre, the leap and lift
reflexive as religious exercise, condition this moment.
On pointe, we are all sore-footed pilgrims performing as
our bloody footprints dry already from dressing room to stage.

RISK MANAGEMENT

History's sculptors released their gritty gods
and animals, grimace of prayer and chisel,

avoiding faults. On pedestals
eroded figures hunch in stone,

the subjects subdued in museums.
Hammered and priceless, immortal and harmless,

none may be rained on, or touched
by exhaust or imprecation, nor lived among.

A LONG ENGAGEMENT

Tickbird sits in Rhino's ear: *trik-quiss*, her hiss
and crackling sets his very horns on edge. She plucks
and crushes ticks, then sips the opened wound,
beak pressed to blood, blood the better food.
But what symbiosis is utterly benign? Who
wants myth's arrangement falsified by fact?

BIOPOIESIS

for creative writing students

You wish the ancients' tricks were so easy still:
Bury a young bull (which first you'll have to kill).
Be sure his horns poke through, above the ground.
Let pass one month; check back as bees surround

the stinking mush from which they seem to rise. Alive
with fresh direction now, they build a hive,
select their queen, make royal jelly—muse;
they dance in air a map, or perhaps a ruse.

The nectar quest will turn their sips to food
that makes more food to sweeten and do good
your midnight heart as it weighs a slaughtered bull
against a swarm against gold drizzled toast. Call

this sequence "causal fallacy," *post
hoc,* yet between us, isn't most
of what we trust a mystery? Our faith
in one wildly written life revitalizes death.

HOW IT BEGINS

At two, you learn to mulch short rows beside the stone fenced orchard.
   Your parents fork then rake through compost, easy in their chores until
      startled by a shadow twitch, your mother ekes out

the name of your father who, now unfocused, lifts his head, as her keen edge
   guides his gloved hand courageous toward the sunny stripe that parts
      rye grass from granite. One foot long, the dangled snake reveals

its copper back, its belly private crimson. Toddle a fresh furrow,
   earnest in your boots. You lean in to kiss what you hadn't known was there.
      Close by, the apple trees hum, your mother's bees fuss in the petals.

NEAR THE END

of the Periodic Table, #79

The Golden Years do
bare ghastly elements
vastly attractive to

rejuvenating ads:
face filled in
by botulinum toxin

or spackle. Truss,
sling flab and that
floppy wobbleneck.

What droops firms
by goop, whitening
for yellow feet and teeth.

Sallow cheeks sag on
jaws now jowly,
hold their own classed by weight

as gold, we know, is. Atomic
Number 79. Pronounce aloud
its symbol, Au. *Awww.*

On another table, fill with awe
your bowl, the late fruit a little
soft on the surface. A windfall.

MAY CONTAIN A GEODE

$5.99 per rock in this bin

The odds are 80/20. Not every one's a winner. Each the size
of your father's closed hand. History opens like a cave,
a mind, more rock. Your geo-tool is close. You've chosen
not to open the rock. You already know past the crust
what you've seen in field guides, memoirs, museums. It's there
you believe, caught you believe in every closed hand, wave
or particle, the light just for you undisclosed.

INEXPRESSIBLY

Of course that's how silence reveals itself.
I want to hear it but there's the beep
of a forklift in reverse; there's the ringing
in my ears. A bug crashes against my
daughter's high frequency curls.
Refrigerated food breaks down despite the cold
and there's the deafening deconstruction

of this make-do bookmark, this postcard written
by my mother days before she died. In church
the interpreter wears solid colors, a curtain
behind her hands' deft evocation of God
whose beguiling privacy unsettles
the heart, the "lub" addressing its twin,

the other side of the river
where women wash work clothes, the shift-change
siren of sweat released into larger bodies
of water, where a sister's hand will slap
the surface, introduce rhythm by skipping a beat.

THRESHOLD

Let a fast place, with one door, enclose thee.
        —Rule of St. Columba

Atop a wave, a narrow door floats—blue
against the lake's own blue. It seems a test: what
pitches toward shore meaning more than nothing,

or less? The ex-nun's here on fall retreat,
to learn among her chaste and faithful friends
what God and she might ask for at this point.

The blue door bobs to flash a bit of brass,
a glinting hinge or knob or fish. A swell
rehangs the door. The lock's still on.

The lower panel's blown, perhaps kicked in,
or thrown by weather up against a rock,
flipped over time itself the open frame.

TIMING

Late, the swimmer flips from the board into the diving well
as the Country Kissin' radio blares: *This is the moment
you've been waiting for.* Not knowing she was supposed
to wait, she kicks, sounds, clicks like a beluga.

Never at home on the surface, she wriggles,
rubs her cap-knobbed head on the drain grate
12 feet down. Goggle-eyed, she stretches
the length of her white body extending back

epochs when the breathless elders' stubby legs stumped up
onto their arctic beach; when lolling in air, blowholes
sandy, the whole pod flipped and sang till—oh!—the life
guard blows the whistle. Out of time. She has to return

to the radio, leaping across stations, picking up sound waves,
grace notes, off; a fluke then, the unexpected depths of silence,
another moment she hadn't known she was waiting for.

LANDSCAPE OF THE MIND

Wit-struck, the mind takes a stride off the side of its boat,
the *Tempus Fugit*. Don't look down, says the divemaster.
Watch the horizon. Eight hours into this twelve-hour drive,
It's all horizon, geological forms that undulate, thrust,
and flatten as they did when this was a nameless stretch
of seabed. Cholla pointed back to bottle sponges,
tumbleweed, corals, lavender, and plankton brushed
mesa tops. This submersible I'm driving, finless, on I-40
is an egg-laying 45-foot marine lizard's hallucination.

As she is mine, tired from steering only forward. Doing
nothing, the mind invents, populates its landscape out of
its briny past. Even when there's no wind, currents carry
the remnants of old storms. Wreckage scoots me a little
toward a trench. Above, the blue surface, where foam rolls
spray and spindrift, breakers spill, darkening cumulus.
The evening rain's begun. Eighteen-wheelers light up;
RVs fishtail in their wake; I turn on my headlights. White-
knuckled, off cruise control, don't stop. At the critical depth,
diver, by breathing you can maintain neutral buoyancy.

AMBIVALENCE

Strong currents and prudence push me back
on board while my scuba group continues its night
drift down toward the channel open at 60 cold feet.
Tank and mask stashed, on the boat bench I lie
on my back, shifting between their line of flashlights
sinking a circle in the deeper dark and up here
this shatter of stars, dry to the touch, and closer.

WHOSE EXPECTATION

Exhibition of a Rhinoceros at Venice (1751)

Commissioned to paint her in situ, Pietro Longhi is sketching
downstage the sturdy Indian Clara: her dimpled vertical folds,
her riveted armor of skin. Wheat straw's in a loose pile,
a few gold shafts in her mouth as if birdlike she's making
a nest that edges off the frame; piling out the other end,
a mound of offal like loaves city birds expect to pick through
after the show. Brought to entertain the borghese of Venice,
she's a curiosity in an age of curios, entitled ladies in pleats
and dominoes, tricorn hats. Clara's horn detached; in his right
hand, her keeper Douwemont Van der Meer waves it and a whip,
a relic and threat in a city awash in Christian body parts.

It's *carnivale* when citizens demand what's unexpected.
Patrons pay artists to render a record shaping what
later they cannot believe they saw. All Clara's years,
watched and crated, she's made her expectations clear.
Venetians in galleries with elegant disgust regard how
she enjoys what she is given, her usual post-show meal:
oranges, tobacco, a bottomless bucket of warm Dutch beer.

THE EX-NUN, UNBURDENED

CAVE CANEM: Beware of the dog
<small>FOUND IN MOSAIC ON ANCIENT ROMAN PORTICOES</small>

Pregnant Blessed Jane, St. Dominic's mother, dreamed
she would bear a son: a dog with a torch in his mouth
to enlighten God's world. *Domini canis.* Beware.

The ex-nun took in not a dog of the Lord, but a stray
of inelegant heritage, mostly Aussie with a taste for deterrents,
tabasco, liquid flame on wood: chairs, gates, threshold.

Basil his name: Doctor of the Church; a fox
in her daughter's library book; choice herb, bushy, short-lived.
Basil of the patchwork eyes, white invading the iris.

What did he see, blanking so, this patristic mutt
who mocked her orthodox bounds by eating her peppery fence?
Who jingled with love and pee'd and pee'd on the carpet, despite?

En route to the pound, Basil unloaded and rolled in the wasted
back seat. His final gesture a chili-rich smear, spicy splinters
of bookcase, Aquinas undigested. Oh Lord, a dark dispensation.

SUB

My whole life I've been a sub, took this
job nearly forty years ago when the real
teacher moved and I was flattered and broke.

Who's been doing my work while I've covered
for quitters, resigned, and absent?
Who covers for me now and what are they

paid? What are their hours? Can they afford
exotic vacations, more personal days—
and how do they dare take my personal days?

In the dark of night, I know myself to lie abed
at prayer; for whom? Who is the I who knows
who prays? It's getting urgent. What comes next

when I put down the briefcase, the grade book
and glasses? For whom do I retire and where?
On their 401(k), I'm stuck in the house

that's never been home while I've maintained
and paid off their mortgage, got siding though
vinyl if final doesn't substitute for wood. Would

they want me to pull a few weeds while I wait
for them to come plant their permanent gardens?
I hope they don't have pets; good Lord, I don't
want to walk their dogs in this late spring rain.

NOT QUITTING ADULT TAP

The proper subject of dance is movement.
   —JOAN ACOCELLA

When the studio texted her I'd quit, my teacher leapt to her feet.
I'd just finished dinner with plenty of wine, settled down reading
that reading contracted our world: from audition to abstraction,
onto the page. How the alphabet focused perception from ear
to eye, so the self had new fixed boundaries, withdrawn
to the literal private, off-stage. Dark and cold and almost time

for the class I'd just quit, the doorbell rang. My God, my teacher!
Said she'd choreographed an old tap routine revamped
for me. Her plan, to keep it simple, counterpoint to mine. She knew,
it's true, I'm crazy for percussion, for soft shoe and classic sounds
of *brush* against, *click* among confident women who tap, but

tell that to this mind perceiving through ears that only half-hear,
to a body tethered by decades, to *shuffle-ball-change*, to *cramp-
roll* and *pullback* and *peri*damn*diddle*. I've stood at the barre, back
to the wall of blabbermouth mirrors. Prompts return to the ear
through the feet, ankles wake up, tight pelvic sockets shriek loose.
I tell myself I can. Or could. Or quit.

She paces, a roll call on my porch, castanet car keys, ready to rumble.
Basic steps keep me upright in motion. The heart itself pumps at
a don't-stop rhythm. I tap into that, eyes closed, strap on my character
shoes without the words—*grab-off, chasse,* and *whatever's next*
in the sequence that trips me up. When I try to read the story I'm in,
I don't want to know how it ends. So, listen—I'm buckling

myself into her car. The *time-step* begins on the last beat
of what might be, okay, the next-to-last step.

MID-LIFE, THE EX-NUN'S BODY
TELLS THE TRUTH

The symptoms suggested hiatal hernia: difficulty breathing,
sense of fullness in the chest. Something bulging undigested.
Heart burn? No, though that area seemed warm;

it wasn't love, but oh, the flutterings and intermittent
hum. The radiologist had been her student once. He'd dated
her daughter, knew of her past, and on occasion prayed
while touring convent ruins on Umbrian vacations.

She drank the barium for a cineradiograph, watched her movie
as it rolled, zoomed, enlarged, then froze as she exhaled.
A study in withheld response, he traced monastic points:

detailed masonry under scaffolding of ribs, past curtains
of lungs. Around the courtyard, bronchial trees,
the lime-white cloister walk; in contrast, he circled
its central depth, that blood-well and fountain, her heart.

Zoom, enlarge. A veiled vessel straightened, smoothed her cape,
waved. The sister had caught a fish or held an invitation, watched
her watcher's awe. Those eyes, the ex-nun's own, looked
at her and looked right back. And looked at her with love.

The ex-nun left the hospital, drove this knowledge home.
At the kitchen window, she reflected through her photogenic body:
Flesh and mortar, inside stories, fill up with light.

She blessed that Motherhouse by heart and drew
inside unruptured life her providential breath.

Her sisters for centuries were hastening to chapel,
under her collarbone, beneath her perfumed breasts.

ONE OF THE PRACTICAL MYSTICS

On reading Margaret Ebner, c. 1300

No Magi clomping down the spotless cloister
hall, no Holy Family packing up for flight.
Past Epiphany, it's just the sculpted Baby
who lies in Margaret's cell.

Candles glow, their miracle of beeswax
melting into wings around the Infant. Now,
urgently incarnate, he's fussing in his alabaster hay.
On hearing—look—the nun unties her gown,

draws her shawl across the gap between what
we can see and what she means to do. One could
name it more than need, but no one else is there,
a stone cold baby's crying—what should a busy
woman offer but a sweet, her own, the overflow?

SAINTS AND AIN'TS

Bearing whatever the iconographers need
to make nametags, the canonized rush to the picnic.
Margaret and her hem-biting dragon on a leash;
Catherine like a schoolgirl rolls her spiked hoop.

Roch's oozing thigh seats him at the end
near Damien who counts off his fingers—
one, two—in the soup. The saints who died
by lumber and tools build their own booths
under T-squaring Joseph, their foreman.
Steaming Martha wears a hairnet to serve.

I want to take their pictures, record how they eat,
if they eat and what, after kissing the handy
lesions of the poor. Anorexics, domestics,
fat Thomas Aquinas, Teresa from the Catskills
of Avila always making with the jokes. Arms
dribbled with birdshit, Francis comes dancing
like Vitus with a rosebush. It's a litany, this family
album. And it's ours. Virgins, martyrs. From the desert,
a flirtation of abbas and ammas. Levitator, seer,
a golden-hearted dullard about to make a speech.

Unprovoked, somebody pitches fireworks
from the other side of the fence. So this is a real
family. Did you expect—be honest—peace?
Did you imagine there wouldn't be a fence?

THE COMIC BAZAAR

At Planet Comicon, the ex-nun processes up aisles
of zealots, hawkers, temples of T & A and gore
in every tongue, understood. The misshapen,
the off-prints, the variants are never discounted.
Spirited heroes kick at their shrink-wrap, call and
mock the average buyer (twelve in the head, all boy,
temptable and under-employed).

The anomalous ex is looking for something like
a reason for being here. She's not read comics for
a biblical forty years yet feels called to this display
of pyro-daydreams, details for sale. Field work,
she'd say, in Babylon. The everywhere expatriate.

The hall expands vast and fluorescent, conventioneers'
faces flensed by illumination aimed to enhance story-
lines, frames, and panels for purchase.
On library tables, their characters altered to products,
writers and artists sell even their ink, their pens,
old templates—now second-class relics.

In a dim corner booth, an action figure
glows in the unholy dark. Because she can,
the ex-nun buys it, takes it home for sanctuary.
A novice, it enters her convent collectibles,
their tabletop cinctured by rosary beads like
votive lamps. Lights-out, the pale green tableau
fades, the liberation in the spending.

CAMOUFLAGE

On the convent dresser her headgear rests,
a miniature theater, with its starched valance
the forehead band, its linen sides like curtains,
the gusset at the neck a tucked proscenium.

Pinned down in the morning, the veil rides upright.
The band makes a shell-thin callus across the nun's
simian ridge, ends before the ears where hair no longer
grows, temples bare after all these years.

Its falling weight opens the gap for seculars to peek inside
between the stiff and the soft, face-framing wimple.
It's called a window, Sisters. Keep yours closed.
The arthritic nun still tries, certain the taut gesture is

futile, certain too that grace builds on humor. To wit,
when the curious peek, they see not hair but goose down.
She has tucked into her window small feathers, from
the Holy Spirit, in truth, her comforter.

"AND AFTER THIS, OUR EXILE. . ."

for the prisoners who discussed Pilgrim at Tinker Creek *with me*

The ex-nun clutched, coasted into the stark
monastic drive, where Security said,
"By tomorrow, spoke and wrote, ma'am,
it's your name'll be all over this place."
Inside the prison, she follows a man with a gun,
a librarian. She knows this life, the worst novitiate

days, nights, a cell in a desert, the death throes
of boredom. Called, she'd answered, sure. Once
for the sake of her soul, now for a book discussion.
The ex has dressed—no make-up, no fragrance—
a deliberate nun again in sturdy shoes, jumper

bound and bagged. In early monastic culture,
even the desert was too confining for a woman
among men. Confused with students, brothers,
these men have shot, cut, raped the people
they look like. Tonight they've prepared Annie Dillard.

One man says nature is the bug on his leg
in bed: "I feel her crawling between the hairs;
when I cup her, I know something bad."
One desert father left his cell with serpents to guard
his provisions. Between charge and sentence,
one boy's godmother offered a day in the arboretum,

another unnatural enclosure.
A desert mother passed as male until her corpse
disclosed those breasts, admired as "withered leaves."
An inmate fools with his belt, mimes rolling his pantleg
to cross a creek. Another mentions the frogs
in The Yard: "To stomp them, you got to be quick."

Trays of cookies arrive under plastic. When one monk
visited another, God's desert raven delivered a doubled
loaf of bread. The apprentice baker stares at crumbs,
chocolate on the apprentice carpenter's table. Territory.

The ex-nun deserts the imprisoned. An educated woman
among men of action, a pilgrim herself, she prays for all
on the dark road home. She knows something natural is
still behind the grille; a paper towel of cookies on the seat
rides, as they say, shotgun.

FELIX CULPA

The snake vertebra's finely worked as porcelain,
hummingbird-shaped—its long beak lifts,
brief wings less bone than whir.

Between beak and rudder, wing and wing,
it's hollow where the spinal cord threads
down the ex-nun's turning back.

She's had her day in the sun. She no longer
hoods nor coils. Neither does she retract.

She hums. Her own vertebrae stack up, give her
the backbone she needs to shiver and heat the air
she perches on, sucking sweetness from an offer

to be like God. She'd do it again. Who could
refuse? In the deep curve of the ruby hibiscus,
who in the world would ask to let this cup pass?

WHAT WORLD DO YOU WANT

The tulip world. Husk and bulb
winter over under ground
yet premature always this green
shock of shoot through leaf mash
blown snow and slush brew.
Now muck then a cup of color,
say, curiosity first, then praise.

BUCKLED UP IN THE BIBLE BELT

The lexicon of Kansas is weather,
a vocabulary of extremes, of expletives
that teach the stranger, the native the local

vernacular for heaven-sent: draught, blizzard, sizzle, ice,
the out-of-this-world gypsy word *tornado* that flings a car over
a trailer park and leaves unbroken one colored egg in its frazzled

basket six feet from where the kitchen was this morning.
I have lived too long in extremis to bother with what
insurance covered and might have replaced, for example

the camera gone back to its maker, its blown roll nearly finished
with shots of model gardens, our bed, the girls at Easter,
their startled dresses, hair gone limp, under a green, uplifting sky.

AFTER PARIS AFTER 40

In a late spring downpour, I jump the gutter—small *arc*
de triomphe—and turn 40. My own Gitanes too soggy to smoke,
I inhale the café's blue on the Champs-Elysees, Elysian
Fields, the exotic afterlife I expect to commence after 40

years of this one. By evening the avenue will shine,
dust and dog ordure rinsed from crowned cobbles; umbrellas,
scarves straight from Hermès, limp luxuries, these kites
of youth. I spring for a second blanc cassis, thumb francs

the color of sand, plum, hedge apple, flip faces of painters,
composers, a physicist, her curls radiant, *le petit prince*
at the watermark. Next week, not in these fields,
my dour money converted, I will backslide, stoic

Kansan at home in sun- and patch-burned pastures.
A woman of a certain age, I'll stand still, let the native
prairie chickens inflate their shocking orange necks
as they boom and strut between bluestem and hayseed.

INVENTION

—Chartres

In the portal of creation, God is being entertained.
He faces forward into aeons we will call our past.
So far, He is amused by this device of balance.

Peering over God's draped shoulder, near His age
about the eyes, a man too new for facial hair looks into
what he'll call the future. Souvenir postcards claim:
"While watching birds, God has the idea of Adam."

No sculptor left a story set in stone for Eve. Alchemists
and glaziers opened masonry to light: three blown roses
in gentle conversation, colorful mouths filled with people.
In the dark swathe under Mary's throat, just above her Baby,
there, in the leadwork's niche, every spring, a nest.

FOLLOW THROUGH

Fruit, it seems, perfects
the branch. Canceled
stamps on aerogrammes
perfect a mailbox
overseas. A crease
in the forehead perfects
a worry as bells
perfect the evening
air. Heel, ball, and all ten
toes: the cupped footprint
perfects the runner's beach.
Crow droppings on my
black car perfect the bird.

OF SOUND MIND AND BODY

A fleece wrapper around the knot, there to protect
the hands of the monk who tolls the bell.
Middle-aged, ropy, he collects himself

for balance, sandaled feet on the ground,
steady in the body's atmosphere
of ease and pleasure and of pain's interruptions.

He's been himself a country at war, unwell.
The bell tolls through organizing air, a wave
that works through the muscles a rhythm:

sound, release, tense; repeat.
The monk measures his resistance to pull again,
having unwrapped the fleece to be stung by hard hemp

bristles that wire him to the task at hand. He squats
to hold the rope taut, then stands to let it all go.
Vibration and whatever lives in the belfry
continue the drama of flight and repose.

STITCHES

The phantom pinching wakes her still,
that pull and twitch years later after a bad dream
of faith in surgery. The scar's lumped up, keloid,
a dermal extravaganza, the nerves haywire nearby.

Her books in anthropology don't lead her back
to sleep. *Some social groups slice themselves*
and stuff their gristly swells of fibroblasts and skin
for ornament. She turns off the light. She'd expected
something thin, perhaps a silver tally mark but dainty.

A scar says you've been pulled together,
or something of you has. Over time
it's like a sunset, the slash of color
drawing down the night to meet the light's
last ray. What is it in the body so drawn
to reconcile and still so insistent on the split?

JERUSALEM PILGRIMAGE, SOUVENIR, 1863

Inside his well-lit shop on Christian Street,
dark-tanned Jacob, a Copt, himself a priest
of sorts sorted his olive wood stencils,
strapped the English girl's arm to a board, then
spread the dyes, the fine needles, giving her
some time to reconsider permanence.
She did not flinch as he drew the blue-black
lines of the Cross. What could her father say?
Last year the Prince of Wales was tattooed here,
same sign. Good for business, thank you, Jesus.

She had heard at home of a sideshow girl
covered in lives of the saints, stained glass scenes,
skin illuminated like medieval
vellum: vines edging her shoulders, scarlet
birds, curls of gilt incense and burnt offerings.

This girl wants a small Jerusalem cross
inside her pale wrist, the sky's after-dusk
blue of summer by the river at home,
where veins branch off, redirect her vision—
no longer the way—to redirect her.
Precisely and fast Jacob worked. Soon, she
could cover the wound with fragrant salve, cloth.
She wouldn't inspect what she'd agreed to.
For the rest of her long-sleeved life, she knew,
it should surprise her, what she paid for.

PASTORAL

The heart is but a small vessel, yet
there are lions: Saint Macarius
in his homily, of the heart. Home,
hot, I open my upper chamber door,
its frame swelled tight; I squeeze outside.

At the far end of here, bees tease out
an orchard. Closer, the gardens thrive;
inedible weeds feed cheaply the fowl
confounded by flung greens, ecstatic
at beetle and grub, just cause for cocky

hosannas or fights. There's a stone wall.
Goats clamber, boulder to bucket,
defy again the electrified fence,
catch with both horns their browse, the fruit
tree's overhang. Macarius follows:

rough uneven roads; there are
precipices in the heart. Even
in my state, flat as a sermon, wind.
Heartland weather's precipitous,
roughs us up, indifferent. Or strategic.

Because *There also is God, the life*
and the kingdom, the light which I'm free
to blow out, withdraw into the dark, snug
fit for a smallish vessel, still allowing for,
you know, some lions.

ST. ANTHONY ABBOT TEMPTED BY A HEAP OF GOLD

Master of the Osservanza Triptych, c. 1435

The way is strewn with rocks.
His tau crutch balanced,
he ignores a grand church.
Trees like black antlers
crack the crags along the path.
Two black birds sit on the still air
behind his thoughts.

At the bend in the road
the abbot halts, directs his stare
as the crouched hare stares
at the scumble where a vandal
scraped the panel of the heap
of gold that was there, is now bare,
as empty as it would have first appeared
to the holy one with the frizzled beard.

WHAT CAN BE PICTURED

Above the page's script like a superego
on his fat belly lies a cherub, one
dimpled knee drops through the *Libera me*.
The phrases age, oak and iron-gall.
Some monk once banked the sides with lapis,
brass; censers' twining smoke curls up edges.
Superior, the cherubs' eyelids droop, drowsy.

Along the manuscript's inferior border
a garden ends medievally in cattails.
Before them a busy second cherub already
clutches in his right hand the plump white
rabbit's ears. He reaches left for the darker
one that's poised to flee and so it must be
he the cherub wants.

Between the justifying claws of marginal
hairy predators, both rabbits turn toward
what's assumed to be a chubby innocent.
Caught by an angel, the white hare's
goodness is a cliché. What makes
the darker turn to sniff his captor's hand
before bolting is not.

ILLUMINATING

Her brothers complained: she is slow at sowing, spinning,
harvest. No one will want her and we—Of course, she

had willed her own slowness: she'd broadcast seeds like
real news, made fog in her fingers with carded wool,

savored the seventh (she being the seventh) of every little
ripeness. Her father gave her to St. Agnes Convent

dowry and all to save her, easy in her aimless life,
insure his family's eternity. An artist, she was attracted

to tools of light and line, the apothecary's pigments, and
perhaps his son, perhaps some Other, like mortar, pestle.

Twenty years later, she's the best. Another lamb,
vellum cured, lines cut, scriptorium-stretched page

across her desk, ready for the uncial she'd dreamed:
capital C for *cor meum*, or was it her father's heart, where

it started. She'd paint that heart true red, the color best
served by a green of ground parsley like garnish on a paten

flat as the world, though growing or plucked, the herb's
edges are frilled as flattery, so-called an aid to digestion.

RENAMING THE PARTICULARS

Pope Gregory conflated three women in history. Ex cathedra,
at that distance, ecclesial logic bargained the lot. Demoniac
with seven devils, contemplative alter-Martha, and harlot of
the toweling long hair: three Bible Marys as one. Just like that.

The tri-femme cruised to Marseilles, preached like sirens
the perfumed gospel, docked, then drew themselves up
to a cleft in the mountains where smelling of thyme and
lavender, daily angels expressed them to heaven to chant

the Hours. Raiment gone to rag, she or they dressed
only in hair, streaming above the treeline, to join as
soprano, second, alto—three ways she or they sang up
their polyphonic God. He or They thundered, spoke,

chirped canticles right back. A crowd, a pride,
an exaltation—three couples in love. They make
the sky at Vespers blush. This visionary pope,
Gregory, in gratitude as one, they renamed "the Great."

GOING THROUGH HISTORY

The ex-nun studies a book on early convent music,
though why should she care about *seicento* Bologna,
suppressed polyphony accompanied by those fierce
hormonal wranglings of abbess and archbishop?

Because this is a book about fighting, which could be useful
at work. It's also about money, so nothing has changed:

Where is God? Donna Lucrezia's motets rise above
the piazza like birds to be clerically shot. Donna Cecilia
weeps in her bed; Donna Louisa beneath her provides
what God and man do not. The ex-nun does not
see a way out of the fatal dailiness and wishes,

wishes she had a TV, a film with its sure and final scene.
In Milan, the nuns wrote Dialogues, musical questions or
conflicts with pull-out-the-stops resolutions. Long solo lines:
This is what I said! Yes! This is what I meant! And refrain
after refrain, until it seems, oh God, a habit of refraining. But
for the finale, the choir bursts, *tutto*, into a splurge of alleluia,

their favorite way in and out of season to end it all, the old
prohibitions against pride humbled again by music.
When Donna Isabella practiced, lay people flocked to the cloister.
Her novitiate dowry had included the illicit trombone, that male
voice, slick slide, the distortion of the brass player's face
contra naturam. Oh, says the ex, the way out has always been.

The single girls next door slim to aerobic recordings.
Rain on the window breaks down its own spectrum.
She tips back her glass and history spills in, such impermanent
boundaries, time, the vows, the music through walls.

ON VISITING CARTHAGE

In high school Latin, I first read Augustine and wary
could not, even threatened by grades, be made to care
for his florid rhetoric or thieving of pears.

Uphill I trudge from the Antonine baths Augustine
must have known. The basement remains where puddles
reflect fallen columns, their leafy capitals upside down.

A corner maquette under glass and condensation shows
to scale the original multi-storied affair, roofed, planted,
ageless. I steal tesserae. Traffic slows,

trips over wrecked mosaic. Stone chips mimicked soft
patterned carpets, camel saddle blankets, slate against
those brilliant tent reds, the nomads' portable craft

then grouted indoors, exclusive once it was called art.
Unpaid workers fashioned pieces, spread them—curved
dolphins, vipers, tridents—to fit trays and to cart

each puzzle, room by echoing room. They knew the work would
last. I admire what I can, aware no slave would have cared for
just another foreigner who occupied a place because she could.

Human history's not far gone. Disposable cameras, escorts shown
to best effect near the *tepidarium*, an old bishop whose *tolle et lege*
still shapes the warp of the West. So many pieces set in stone.

WHY OBEDIENCE IS THE ONLY VOW

At the flea market, the ex-nun ignores
a taxidermist's shadow box: one stuffed

finch grips the broken spine of a field
guide. Dynamics of flight insist

upon resistance; a perch too flexible
won't let a bird take off.

ENCLOSURE, REVISED

That feminist summer in Bible school,
the deliberate and recent ex-nun, still
rankled by Latin, translated: no longer
"a garden enclosed," *hortus conclusus*
will mean (whorish conclusion) profusion
not walled or made fussy or watched.

Not even in a dictionary does profusion
follow surveillance, though to precede is not
to preclude. Achievement and humility, say,
could mate in any language where blossom
and dirt ignore what they're called.

Thus did she continue creating her translation:
This garden kicked up its heels, bright vines
bound rake to hoe to wall that grew itself
porous as logic. Mortar blushed and lichen
textured the wild facade. Buckets rested
unto rust. She puzzled out herself: here

what found the sun did not fail to thrive, and
what failed fell apart until the parts formed
one humorous earth. Honeybee
and stamen and pistil—here
grace built on nectar—a golden heart,
a *hortus*, the ex-nun concluded, *profusus.*

THE EX-NUN DOES
NOT CONSIDER REJOINING

A raccoon's corpse rests, its long hand bones still
articulated. Tendons, ligaments of water-weed
under a lap robe. Abysmal, an invalid's day at the shore.

The robe is matted, a drying felt of flotsam and the fur
which the instant before death had rippled against
the sensation of swimming. Certainly,

the animal had been hungry, fishing at the mouth
of a river alive with Coho and over-reached into the current
in the play, the life, of need, of far-fetching need,

the very current which once swept away two splashing
children and the athletic witness who dove to their rescue
and drowned, all three, in wildly indifferent water.

One can drown in such familiar elements. Near a point
farther down the beach, a gull rolls in the shallows,
its wingspread mottled, logy, head bowed too long.

THE EX-NUN VOLUNTEERS ON THE DIG

Dix Pit, Stanton Harcourt, Oxfordshire

Pull the trowel straight toward you, she's told.
What you've chipped, a curator will have to turn,
to hide, to name "point of discovery."
Thirty years ago, she would've had to act grateful
for the correction, would've had to wear
the offending trowel, the wreckage, around her neck,
to sit for meals on the floor in the midst of her sisters,
not turned away but serving as point of discovery.

She had not imagined the work this would be—
dressing in sweats, her habit, warm
under Mary-blue raingear streaked
quarry-orange, the mismatched Wellies—
every wet day for a fortnight. Aeons drop through
gravel to clay to a mammoth's partial pelvis
shaped like a bicycle seat, a bison metatarsal
seeming mahogany, a clawfoot
table leg. The part representing the absent,

the wholly other, of two thousand centuries
ago. Tedious as novitiate and as silent, disciplined
by rain and superiors. Trowel, bucket, kneeler,
equipment named like religious goods: surveyors'
theodolite. What else but a god's little telescope
checking up? It sites her bearings, coordinates.
It measures exactly where she is and is not. She asks
for confirmation before she makes her mark; no chance
to erase on the damp, flannel-soft chart.

She squints at the sieve where she's shaken a bucket,
thinking she'd seen something. Tired, unable to find it again,
she weeps, or it is rain washing the matter through mesh.
Ah, a freshwater fish vertebra, a second pine nut
the size of a freckle. She brushes her face, the screen,
the Chapter of Faults: scruples, hundreds of
thousands of years swept along, tumbled tiny,
shining here where once a river went way out of bounds.
Heavy mammals taking drinks with their young were taken

by surprise, split up by wet force overflowing its banks.
Whirlpools and undertows no one can chart.
The ex-nun flings her trowel, point down, till it sticks

like a knife in soft dirt. She crosses the dump site.
Gulls ride thermals over burst and rotting garbage,
the bin bags so blue along that ridge,
surely some sky must have fallen.

ATTENDING TO REMAINS

Forensic science scrubs the skull smooth as old ivory,
the plates so attached in their roundabout seams
one could miss the connection to art, to piano keys
and scrimshaw. A carver could scratch his own head
and etch the story inside this bowl of bone
with stick figures like thoughts: a girl giving up
everything to live here. Fish in the currents.
Seaweed maybe; fish have to eat. Firewood,
and a library far enough from it just for the light.
The rest of the body's dried pulp in long bones
sounding of low tide flutes; the obvious xylophone
ribs with variable mallets; pelvic ledgers scored;
tchotchkes. When the fire's high, teeth crowned
reflect a culture's treasure. And dice, carved
even poorly, roll out what the bones have
ever been beneath it all, a medium for luck.

THE EX-NUN & THE PRIEST:
QUESTIONS OF INNOCENCE

The priest's first day of vacation, he phoned her:
Let's meet at the bakery, watch folks go to work.
They did and they did, then walked off their sweet rolls
along the lake shore, past Navy Pier, a bell on each

hour, past the marinas, past all reason—miles
of urban water. What had been cast upon it returned
as printed wrappers, shredding, tattooed jellyfish;
docked, Mozart soloed over brass fittings and foam.

Jesus chose a desert but required too a lake
for his teaching at the margins, his parabolic talks
with fish, the crowds scrappy, the literal net. The priest
willed her away from the edge. I can't swim, he said.

You're clergy, she said. You can walk. And he did,
a little farther inside. Don't blame the church on me.
But I do, she said, herself as well for catechizing all
those years, dispensing stars for answers.

Answers. He stopped, looked past her to the vast
blue, blown gulls low on garbage
or the Holy Ghost. The brown-aired horizon split
like a hair. Forgiveness he could not give her and she

would not accept an answer to a question no child
could ask at seven, the lisp snagging: *What is sin?*
It's a thin line between adventure and fear
laid down like a pier; Father, what has it meant

to tie up here? A call to Profound Silence,
as when bells rang and saved them every evening
of their lives from telling what they longed to have
done. They leaned into the lacuna, their vocations

limning the pilings. Minnows, small change, flashed
through the complexion of shadows submerged,
dispersing themselves around slippery rocks.

THE EX-NUN REMEMBERS THE RULER

Measure up, she tells her children, points
to their rulers, their feet. Pace off the classroom.
The youngest Martinez, whose birth
embarrassed his much older sisters, tugs at
Maria's black braid. *Jesus!*

calls the nun more than once and slaps
up the aisle behind them. *Jesus! Maria!*
Reverting to type, she looms—then laughs.
Some joke, her children, that image.
Called by the bell to change, the class

stretches, up go their rulers wanting to kiss,
to cross like a roomful of Knights
of Columbus, or mutinous slaves,
short oars without paddles,
about to revolt. Have they a prayer?

Over metrics she'd chosen the illogical 12
inch to honor apostles. Considered dividing
the product of 4 x 3 into red-hatted cardinal
directions adjusted by Paul's theological
virtues. And the greatest of these?

After Compline, she paced her own
immeasurable cell, counting on (one foot
after the other) poverty, chastity, obedience,
rounding the corners they could put her in.

THE EX-NUN, PHONICS,
AND THE COMIC BOOK BOY

for Ben Dunn, creator of The Warrior Nun *comics*

She recalls Ben, who might have been a linguist, learning
to spell by sounding out action. THOCK. SSSPT—
with the T nearly silent, his tongue jammed against
the space where his teeth will come in huge as warrior
shields. BRRR does not sound as cold as J-J-J, he says.
And why do French dogs say OUA, not WOOF? Switch
to gore. ZZINGG: the guillotine. THWIK: the arrow's
short flight from string to clean entry. You want blood?

The crucifix. Ben's whole body attends to the sounds
of the dying Christ. Blood from His hands drips in two
(PLIK? PLOK?) puddles; from His feet gravity sluices it
down to the chalk troughs, hissing hot, snakes.
The wound in His side is a dam burst, big vowels, Ben
writes, hugely open, a roar of blood and water landing
on his classmates as they turn in their seatwork.
Oh phonics' gristly gobbets! What is the sound of the lance?
With his sharpened pencil, he pokes his fingertip—
insignificant: *pk, pt.* A lance requires the majesty of physics;
the ribcage of his God, Ben knows, is a soundbox.

SWEEPING THE HEARTH

I praise the split-haired broom,
its homely bristles' curl
attentive to details, ash
remains of last night's blaze:

the leap and lull of a curious love,
its arc, a flame, assumes a pulse
not unlike that other
between our skin and hope.

XO

On what might have been our anniversary

How our desires signed off, stringing along
kisses and hugs. Once a game, an alphabet

for two boxed in pens, our characters
tick-tacked onto a lattice.

I'd x you out. You'd hold your place.
We crossed ourselves, carved the zero

of a face in bank accounts, park benches, sand.
Like hope in deep midwinter, no valentine survives

on frosted windshields, sugar hearts. XO can
disappear, a change not like weather but when,

like a woodcut, the inked vows erode from relief
to vague and slurred impressions. Even kissing

cost us breath; the tight squeeze, breadth.
In grading, lists, the X means wrong and done.

More than binary, O means failed, perfect.

AT KROGER'S, THE DAY AFTER
MY FORMER HUSBAND DIED

A competition choosing avocadoes—
Surprise! The woman offers me herself.
Attention must be given, see, she knows that
something's wrong. It seems she wants to help
me weigh each fruit, black, green rough hide,
the pulp too hard or gone to mush too soon, to rot.
I'm blind to what I feel. My hand's a stump,
my mind too numb to make a choice. I'm not
sure why I came, except some hunger drove
me not to produce but to people, strangers,
store-bought company. I see a guacamole bowl,
a dip to share, but I'm alone, hence caught
by kindness. "How are you?" she asks and looks
inside my blank unbalanced face that brooks
no entry. Yet she enters, rests her ringed hand
light but firm on my arm, no grand gesture.
Who saw this might think her reassurance meant
we're friends, meant not every presence ends.

PREVENIENT GRACE

The day after they'd offered their gifts,
they found the stable empty, there,
where once their light and destination lay.
Through the sable radiance they stared at
one another, acknowledging those travel plans
had been for what they'd brought. And left.
And surely something more,

each thought but didn't need to say aloud.
So long a trip, at first their hunches private,
now three capacious minds a kind of music.
The one leaned tall against the post,
the others spread their brocade on hay
that smelled still of human afterbirth,
milkspray and heavy sleep through which
the same angel who'd wakened them
had made a visitation here.
They turned to divination. The wise and cunning
foresee how homage portends damage.

None sensed a sure way to go home at all
the same, such spirals and meanders, contingencies.
They frowned together down a well deep enough
to see the stars reflect in this day's light.
Not one appeared like yesterday's.
As in the altering nature of all gifts,
they were already being moved along.

NEW YEAR'S EVE, A WAKE

Some weeks dead, he's shifted. Not now
himself this fistful, his broken teeth,
the sifted ash of fascia, nails, beard.

The kiln man will have pocketed splashes of
dental gold annealed on the slab. Spit and fats
up the chimney into air. It's not sublimation.

The air of himself caught in winds off the coast,
blown back across Red and Blue states, mixing it up
in the Rust Belt, down toward Huck's Mississippi

raft high, twisting over the Plains' debris clouds.
He settles once again in his old apartment
to shuffle the virtual deck for Solitaire.

It's not all virtual. Some heft of him remains in a box
on a mantel in Maine. Fine grained wood, a brass
plaque underneath, coasters on his lid, always ready

for a party. At rest in his daughter's low-lit home.
Upstairs, his granddaughters won't stay tucked in.
Downstairs, champagne and fresh arrivals, ruddy

cheeked, a dust of snow on their hat brims,
everyone is urged toward the living room.

THE EX-NUN GROWS RESTLESS AGAIN

under the Zoo & Botanical Gardens' only bo tree.
She's driven there midmorning to sit, half-awake,
half-lotus, before they turn the waterfall on.

Caged capuchins chitter like thoughts.
She roots herself in the zoo's rain forest, illusion
of jungle, to follow her breath. *Not thinking.*

The Buddha bench faces another cage—okay,
the illusion of an other—in which is slung
the tutelary sloth and its three-toed stink.

Sequined apparitions, birds skim the mist. *Thinking.*
Behind her, the pond is pent up till noon, where kissing
gourami, able to breathe air, keep their unnecessary

water awake. Beyond them, a tank of piranhas.
Distracted along the bark-chip path, a rustling
above of leather-caped dogs? Fruit bats! Pointing,

visitors spill their snacks. From careful underbrush,
acouchi scurry out to eat. Popcorn. *Thinking.*
It's not good for them; they love it. The woman, both

legs asleep, prays like a Christian, that is, for an end.
Noon, the keeper opens a valve. The woman's monkey
mind raves at plain water's trained freefall.

HABITUALLY NOCTURNAL AND SOLITARY

The Amur leopard had been textbook readied. The female
joined him on exhibit to be made much of, to make more of.
Sweaty preschoolers at the close of their field trip yawned,
shackled by pink yarn and chaperones. They paused here,
near the drinking fountain under too much pressure, to recount
themselves before, roused, the male roared once and leapt.

The female's blood, her screams, shot through the bars,
arced over the children, one of whose pale parents dropped
to the spattered pavement. Zoo volunteers pruning shrubs
cried out: keepers, security, vets, a helpless human uproar.

The son of the woman who fainted will spend the night
untying the yarn between leap and drop, red blood, flung blood,
the spurt and bubble world gone wild, then limp, so local
he stopped hearing. The leopard's wet jaws, he sees,
will keep working on his mate, widening in that silence.

IMAGINING THE ANTIDOTE

to my species' means to thrive
(guile, lust, preening, cowardice—
the list spreads, splits and ages)
unscientifically I roam the zoo.
A husky elephant trainer whispers,
Wanna cop a feel? meaning to lay a treat
with my whole hand in trunk-uplifted
Simba's mouth. If I say yes, she'll glow
Hindu blue, elongate her earlobes, wave
her many hands full of manifest charms.
She smells of sandalwood and undigested hay.
On the slick pink pillow of her tongue
I plop my hand and a small sweet potato,
an offering the size of, say, a child's heart.

ROUTING

These tangles and plaques say Alzheimer's. *Requiescat in pace*,
the brain of Sister N. sits in a container. Formalin has fixed it
for research, nothing more for her but the clear and eternal. Now

imagine a brain in a plastic tub shipped on the UPS truck next to my
high-fashion catalog choice, the scarf I'll discover so fringed it tangles
with itself, an unforeseeable annoyance. The truck, a modest brown,

bears down the snowy streets, an icon of fulfillment, chock
full of the consequence of choice, and better, of follow-through.
I gave up a life of promise, simplicity, direction, and chose

or was chosen—I want it both ways—to choose me.
In a decade it may be my brain in a bucket, wedged safe,
unaware, in a truck turning the corner.

WHAT'S LEFT

At a conference on art and religion, the ex-nun quits the panels
of academe, visits what's left of the Branch Davidians

by taxi in a late winter drizzle. Not like the slow ruins of abbeys
in Europe, she'd watched this one fall under televised storm.

This afternoon, the cellar of the men's dorm is full of rain,
her face thrown back shattered from the water's surface.

Their tunnels had been sealed. Fire and water, David and God.
In the distance, uncritical cows. Inside the compound, saplings

stand, one each for the dead eighty-plus. Two spots of color:
the teddy bear in jonquils, school-bus yellow, and fading

the plush robin wedged in forked twigs, "Serenity Sea Jones—age 4."
February clouds mumble, evasive. Her tree announces spring

where sacred space isn't so, and religious life continues to fall
under brokered gravity, under fire. An insider once,

the ex-nun's now without a guide in this world, so she observes,
reports the confusion of signs by informants, witnesses.

THE EX-NUN IS IN

the pool with the VA class,
swimming relics of a world
war in their slack breasts, overripe
hands; those scars faded lighter
than tattoos are the old ones.

The new—by-passes, plates,
replacements not done in a field tent—
are nearly invisible as
the men. She calls them all
grandfather. The men flip

flop on yellow feet, a lifetime of
wingtips, steel-toes, cleats, what
they were before they were here
now squinting at what must be her
cleavage, they're sure, the big lugs.

These men in shy boxers
at a pool not a beach head or jungle or
engine or office, they've swum upstream,
awaited some tide to turn all their lives
since the war, their novitiate.

They've slapped Brut on those hang
dog jowls; in chlorine it dissolves,
a chemical weapon. She crawls hard,
gasping, to the farthest edge
before they further trouble the water

so wishing to cannonball flirt, so
headfirst impossible now their knees
don't bend. They scuff down the ramp, tight
to the rail and proud. An underlit pool; easing
up, a wet woman; themselves almost buoyant.

EASTER

Christ in the Desert Monastery

At 3 a.m., the desert is rigor mortis cold.
We seculars, gritty and sleep sour, drive
miles of God's country pot-holes, the Rio

Chama below us crazy with snowmelt and
moon. At the parking lot, headlights
wink out. The faithful find the path carefully

balanced in a darkness heralded and backed by
darkness. Our flashlights snake
between sage and red rock. Hikers' boots

crunch, hush up to chapel, toward the warmest
seats. A novice stokes a piñon stove, passes honey-
sweet tapers. Later, the monks file outside

in the fullness of their insular habits. Hooded
nightbirds. *Who?* they chant. *Who is within?*
They knock on their own doors.

We are two women inside a warming tomb,
mother and daughter, we follow their rite,
sing back, *He is not here.* Yawning,

the eastern horizon brightens
between mountains light as eggs.

THE EX-NUN IN THE NURSING HOME

shares a room with a woman she calls
a feather on God's bad breath, all indigestion
from the tears she mushes into her bread,
her gas could power Detroit. Charity,
the ex-nun prays in her sleep
keeping the other awake enough

to answer her prayers with cursing.
The other dresses floppy and uses
bad grammar. The ex-nun thinks she
should have stayed in the Order, sure now
of a single room down a rubber-soled hall
of educated women too well-known to kill.

She's not thought of the nun of Monza
since 1607, that Lombard Sister Virginia Maria,
her secret lover—Gianpaolo something—
who knifed two sisters before they could snitch,
stuffed a third down a dry well. The woman
in the other bed snores. When the ex-nun hit

menopause, she lost her libido, slept alone
for decades before committing herself to this.
Convents once warehoused women too used or
poor to marry, whether God called them or not.

When the ex-nun had entered, she thought
herself called as those hundred other
working-class girls, high school honors grads
to whom God issued the same invitation and
after some time released less formal retractions.
She could have married a neighborhood boy,

Irish mechanic or entrepreneur who'd end on one side
of bars or the other. She could have had babies,
looked at magazines, slept with a rosary or drunk
Lourdes water and gin. Compare any lad to God. No.
She'd got a new name, a private room, a cloak and
veil, an education. She'd gotten privilege.

She'd gotten out. And what today is that worth?
The price of experience, sister, miss, is incalculable
and going up. She beseeches her aged mate, "Jesus,
death soon, love." Bloody and beat, He seems to nod
like a deaf old Spouse, or nod off, like the other
woman in this cell, whose past is releasing itself.

THE EX-NUN'S DEATH

will not be as she'd imagined. No scythe.
No grim shade turning down the corner
of her page. Not even an angel scrimping
for the day's quota. As a young nun,
she'd drilled 55 frilled and tie-tacked First
Communicants, antsy for gifts, for God,
dropping the kneelers, forgetting again:
Will Jesus bleed if I bite Him? What if I
throw up? She'd laughed, "You kids
will be the death of me!" And here they—

she will lean forward to catch the breath
that will not come, lean to hear each
whisper a family rage or wager or trade
the lunchbag banana. She leans
toward their beaming faces, the pain
in her chest breaching a grimace,
almost a smile. Out of habit
they reach for her, bury their faces
under her ribs as they did before
she knew how near they'd come
to be loved all her life.

WHAT SHE KNOWS

She'll never be old enough, out of this or any habit
so far it all makes sense. She may be shocked
by lightning, loose shingles, a soft shoulder, sufficient
drama to recognize drama as approximate. The messenger
is not the message. The warning is not the tragedy.
Are we saved? asks the dewy-eyed communicant.
We are saved, replies the agnostic wiping her bifocals
on God's soft shirttail, untucked, barely.

SABBATICAL: MORNING AND COMFORT

I have left my job, home, friends; chosen
at a distance, this room I leased, my cell
avails me of an earlier life. I keep custody
of my senses again, rise early, let go of sleep
in candlelight's secular Matins with coffee.

On the other side of our common wall,
my careful landlady descends from
dream to morning rite as if there were
a difference. Once her kettle's filled,
placed on what without her glasses
seems the burner, she will sneeze and
I anticipate another; yes. Then, bounce to

thud, a cupboard door obeys its latch,
suction of the opened fridge, shrill spoon
across the copper countertop. The floor
resists, itself not quite awake, its many tongues
stuck in their habitual grooves. Soon, the pad
of her socks, the chair's slide out then in,
the caw of early birds; pages of newspaper
turn lightly, like leaves, like Lauds.

Acknowledgments

My gratitude to the editors who published these or versions of the following:

Animus: "Enclosure, Revised" and "Invention"

Bellingham Review: "'And after This, Our Exile. . .'," "Threshold," "Routing," "One of the Practical Mystics"

Beloit Poetry Journal: "A Long Engagement"

DoubleTake: "Renaming the Particulars" and "The Ex-Nun & the Priest: Questions of Innocence"

Image: "The Ex-Nun, Phonics, and the Comic Book Boy," "Easter," "The Ex-Nun Is In," "Midlife, the Ex-Nun's Body Tells the Truth," "What's Left," "Echo," "Before Entering"

Northwest Review: "Buckled Up in the Bible Belt"

Poet Lore: "Inexpressibly"

Poetry East: "Illuminating," "Ichthyology," "Why Obedience Is the Only Vow," "Sabbatical: Morning and Comfort"

Rock & Sling: "Felix Culpa"

St. Katherine's Review: "Pastoral"

Sojourners: "Sweeping the Hearth"

Winged: "Biopoiesis"

Finishing Line Press: poems previously published in the chapbook, *The Ex-Nun Poems* (2011)

This book was set in Centaur, designed by the American typographer and book designer, Bruce Rogers, who was commissioned to create an exclusive type for the Metropolitan Museum of Art (New York) in 1914. Based on the Renaissance-period printing of Nicolas Jenson around 1470, it was named Centaur after the title of the first book designed by Rogers using the type: *The Centaur* by Maurice de Guérin, published in 1915. Lanston Monotype of London cut the commercial version of Centaur and released it in 1929.

This book was designed by Ian Creeger, Jim Tedrick, and Gregory Wolfe. It was published in hardcover, paperback, and electronic formats by Wipf and Stock Publishers, Eugene, Oregon.

The cover was designed by Shannon Carter, Jim Tedrick, and Gregory Wolfe.

The cover image is *Exhibition of a Rhinoceros at Venice*, by Pietro Longhi, painted around 1751, and held in the collection of The National Gallery, Washington, DC.